Exploring
CALIFORNIA
MISSIONS

SOUTHERN COAST MISSIONS IN CALIFORNIA

BY
NANCY LEMKE

CONSULTANT:
JAMES J. RAWLS, PH. D.
PROFESSOR EMERITUS
DEPARTMENT OF HISTORY
DIABLO VALLEY COLLEGE

⌐ LERNER PUBLICATIONS COMPANY/MINNEAPOLIS

Lerner Publications Company
A division of Lerner Publishing Group, Inc.
241 First Avenue North
Minneapolis, MN 55401 U.S.A.

Website address: www.lernerbooks.com

Library of Congress Cataloging-in-Publication Data

Lemke, Nancy, 1949–
    Southern coast missions in California / by Nancy Lemke.
        p.   cm. — (Exploring California missions)
    Includes index.
    ISBN-13: 978–0–8225–1935–5 (lib. bdg. : alk. paper)
    1. Missions, Spanish—California—Pacific Coast—History—Juvenile literature. 2. Missions, Spanish—California, Southern—History—Juvenile literature. 3. Pacific Coast (Calif.) —History, Local—Juvenile literature. 4. California, Southern—History, Local—Juvenile literature. 5. San Diego Mission—History—Juvenile literature. 6. Mission San Juan Capistrano—History—Juvenile literature. 7. San Luis Rey Mission (Calif.) —History—Juvenile literature. 8. Spanish mission buildings—California—Pacific Coast—Juvenile literature. 9. Indians of North America—Missions—California—Pacific Coast—History—Juvenile literature. 10. California—History—To 1846—Juvenile literature. I. Title.
    F868.P33L46 2008
    979.4'9—dc22   2006036845

Manufactured in the United States of America
1 2 3 4 5 6 – DP – 13 12 11 10 09 08

CONTENTS

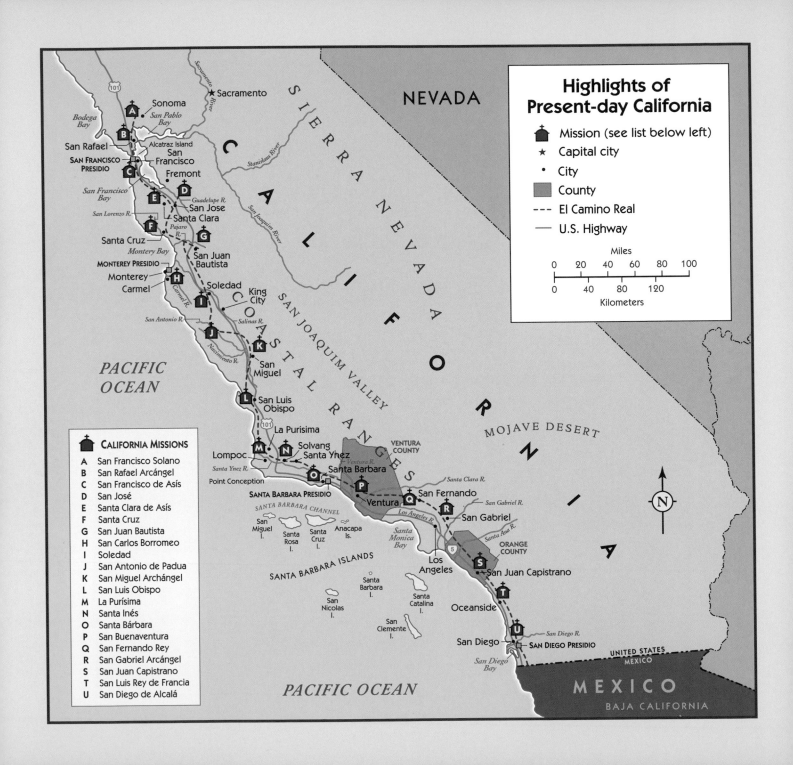

Highlights of Present-day California

- ⛪ Mission (see list below left)
- ★ Capital city
- • City
- County
- – – – El Camino Real
- —— U.S. Highway

Miles
0 20 40 60 80 100

Kilometers
0 40 80 120

CALIFORNIA MISSIONS

- A San Francisco Solano
- B San Rafael Arcángel
- C San Francisco de Asís
- D San José
- E Santa Clara de Asís
- F Santa Cruz
- G San Juan Bautista
- H San Carlos Borromeo
- I Soledad
- J San Antonio de Padua
- K San Miguel Archángel
- L San Luis Obispo
- M La Purísima
- N Santa Inés
- O Santa Bárbara
- P San Buenaventura
- Q San Fernando Rey
- R San Gabriel Arcángel
- S San Juan Capistrano
- T San Luis Rey de Francia
- U San Diego de Alcalá

NEVADA

PACIFIC OCEAN

CALIFORNIA

SIERRA NEVADA

SAN JOAQUIM VALLEY

COASTAL RANGES

MOJAVE DESERT

Sonoma
★ Sacramento
Bodega Bay
San Pablo Bay
San Francisco Solano
San Rafael
Alcatraz Island
San Francisco
SAN FRANCISCO PRESIDIO
Fremont
San Francisco Bay
San Lorenzo R.
Guadelupe R.
San Jose
Santa Clara
Pajaro R.
Santa Cruz
Montery Bay
San Juan Bautista
MONTEREY PRESIDIO
Monterey
Carmel
Carmel R.
Soledad
King City
Salinas R.
San Antonio R.
Nacimiento R.
San Miguel
San Luis Obispo
La Purisima
Lompoc
Solvang
Santa Ynez
Santa Ynez R.
Point Conception
SANTA BARBARA PRESIDIO
Santa Barbara
VENTURA COUNTY
Ventura R.
Santa Clara R.
San Fernando
Ventura
San Gabriel R.
San Gabriel
Los Angeles R.
Los Angeles
Santa Monica Bay
ORANGE COUNTY
Santa Ana R.
San Juan Capistrano
Oceanside
San Diego R.
San Diego
SAN DIEGO PRESIDIO
San Diego Bay

SANTA BARBARA CHANNEL
San Miguel I.
Santa Rosa I.
Santa Cruz I.
Anacapa Is.
SANTA BARBARA ISLANDS
Santa Barbara I.
San Nicolas I.
Santa Catalina I.
San Clemente I.

Sacramento River
Stanislaus River
San Joaquim River

PACIFIC OCEAN

N

UNITED STATES
MEXICO

MEXICO
BAJA CALIFORNIA

INTRODUCTION

Spain and the Roman Catholic Church built twenty California **missions** between 1769 and 1817. A final mission was built in 1823. The missions stand along a narrow strip of California's Pacific coast. Today, the missions sit near Highway 101. They are between the cities of San Diego and Sonoma.

The Spaniards built **presidios** (forts) and missions throughout their empire. This system helped the Spanish claim and protect new lands. In California, the main goal of the mission system was to control Native Americans and their lands. The Spaniards wanted Native Americans to accept their leadership and way of life.

Spanish **missionaries** and soldiers ran the presidio and mission system. Father Junípero Serra was the missions' first leader. He was called father-president. Father Serra and the other priests taught Native Americans the Catholic faith. The priests showed them how to behave like Spaniards. The soldiers made sure Native Americans obeyed the priests.

The area was home to many Native American groups. They had their own beliefs and practices. The Spanish ways were much different from their own. Some Native Americans willingly joined the missions. But others did not. They did not want to give up their own ways of life.

The Spaniards tried different methods to make Native Americans join their missions. Sometimes they gave the Native Americans gifts. Other times, the Spanish used force. To stay alive, the Native Americans had no choice but to join the missions.

The Spanish called Native Americans who joined their missions **neophytes.** The Spaniards taught neophytes the Catholic religion. The neophytes built buildings and farmed the land. They also produced goods, such as cloth and soap. They built a trade route connecting the missions. It was called El Camino Reál (the Royal Road). The goods and trade were expected to earn money and power for Spain.

But the system did not last. More than half of the Native Americans died from diseases the Spaniards brought. Mexico took control of the missions in 1821. Neophytes were free to leave or stay at the missions. In 1848, the United States gained control of California and closed the missions. Some of the remaining neophytes returned to their people. But many others had no people to return to. They moved to **pueblos** (towns) or inland areas. The missions sat empty. They fell apart over time.

This book is about three missions in southwestern California. Spanish missionaries built San Diego de Alcalá in 1769. In 1776, they set up San Juan Capistrano north of modern-day San Diego. Missionaries founded San Luis Rey de Francia in 1798.

CALIFORNIA MISSION	FOUNDING DATE
San Diego de Alcalá	July 16, 1769
San Carlos Borromeo de Carmelo	June 3, 1770
San Antonio de Padua	July 14, 1771
San Gabriel Arcángel	September 8, 1771
San Luis Obispo de Tolosa	September 1, 1772
San Francisco de Asís	June 29, 1776
San Juan Capistrano	November 1, 1776
Santa Clara de Asís	January 12, 1777
San Buenaventura	March 31, 1782
Santa Bárbara Virgen y Mártir	December 4, 1786
La Purísima Concepción de María Santísima	December 8, 1787
Santa Cruz	August 28, 1791
Nuestra Señora de la Soledad	October 9, 1791
San José	June 11, 1797
San Juan Bautista	June 24, 1797
San Miguel Arcángel	July 25, 1797
San Fernando Rey de España	September 8, 1797
San Luis Rey de Francia	June 13, 1798
Santa Inés Virgen y Mártir	September 17, 1804
San Rafael Arcángel	December 14, 1817
San Francisco Solano	July 4, 1823

The rugged California
coast near San Diego

EARLY LIFE ALONG THE COAST

Long ago, southwestern California was much as it is in modern times. The land is rich and varied. The sand and rocky soil of the coast changes inland to canyons, valleys, and flat-topped hills called **mesas**. High foothills and mountains rise up in the east. Creeks and rivers flow down from the mountains through the valleys to the sea. The mountain land drops 6,000 feet (1,829 meters) to a sandy, eastern desert.

Southwestern California has a mild climate. The coast is warm all year. The central area and coastal mountains are

Mountain lions make their homes in southwestern California.

warm in the summer and cool in winter. The mountains receive the most rainfall. The coast and central area receive rain during the rainy seasons each winter and early spring. The eastern desert is hot. It receives little rainfall.

Many kinds of plants and wildlife live in the region. Large patches of chaparral bushes spread over the ground. The scrubby plants thrive in hot summer weather. Chapparal bushes are home to different types of birds. They also make a good place for rabbits, skunks, rats, and lizards to hide. The Pacific Ocean is home to whales, fish, and seals. Inland, mountain lions and deer roam grassy

meadows. Large, twisted oaks rise from the ground. The land slowly rises to rugged coastal ranges. Pine trees join oak trees here. Mountain sheep leap up and down the mountainsides. Coyotes, kangaroo rats, and antelope squirrels live among the thorny cactus and agave plants of the desert.

THE PEOPLE

Native Americans were the first people to settle southwestern California. They came to the area from the north and east several thousand years ago. By the 1500s, about 7,000 Native Americans lived in the region.

The Native Americans of southwestern California spoke forms of two languages. The languages are called Shoshonean (shoh-SHOH-nee-un) and Yuman (YOO-mun). Most Native Americans who spoke the Yuman language settled in groups near modern-day San Diego. Those who spoke the Shoshonean language lived north of the Yuman groups.

These American Indians shared a common way of life. They lived in groups called **bands.** There were about 100 to 500 people in each band. Band members lived in villages. Some bands called themselves "the people" in their languages. Others named themselves after their village names.

NATIVE AMERICAN COMMUNITIES

The Native Americans of southwestern California had their own way of life. It fit the seasons and the environment. Their

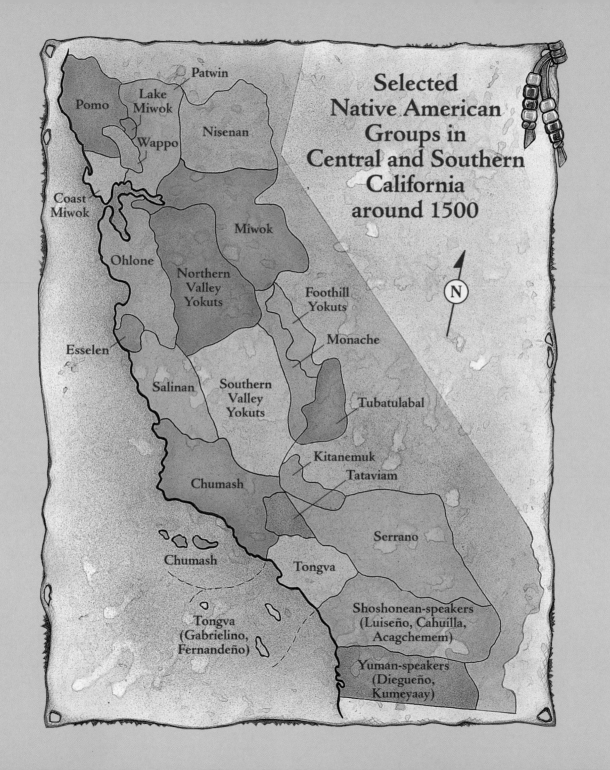

Selected
Native American
Groups in
Central and Southern
California
around 1500

N

Patwin
Lake Miwok
Pomo
Wappo
Nisenan
Coast Miwok
Miwok
Ohlone
Northern Valley Yokuts
Foothill Yokuts
Monache
Esselen
Salinan
Southern Valley Yokuts
Tubatulabal
Kitanemuk
Tataviam
Chumash
Serrano
Chumash
Tongva
Shoshonean-speakers
(Luiseño, Cahuilla,
Acagchemem)
Tongva
(Gabrielino,
Fernandeño)
Yuman-speakers
(Diegueño,
Kumeyaay)

homes, clothing, food, and religion were tied to the land.

American Indians usually set up their villages along creeks or rivers. The creeks and rivers gave them fresh water. The American Indians built dome-shaped homes. They tied willow sticks together to make a frame. They covered the frame with reeds or other grasses. Sometimes they added a layer of soil for more protection. When the homes became old, American Indians burned them and built new ones.

Shoshonean- and Yuman- speakers made their homes of sticks and grass.

These American Indian women are preparing a meal using acorn nuts they gathered.

American Indians in the region usually wore few clothes because the weather was warm. Women dressed in skirts. They made the skirts from reeds, animal skins, or willow bark. Men often wore only belts to hold tools and knives. Many children wore no clothing at all. In cold weather, the people kept warm with animal skin blankets and capes.

The Native Americans fished and hunted animals for food. Hunters stalked birds, rabbits, deer, and other animals. Native Americans also gathered roots, nuts, herbs, and other plants to eat. Acorns were the most important food. These nuts come from highland oak trees. Native Americans went into the mountains to collect acorns each fall. Then they made the nuts into a soft cereal. They ate the porridge plain or flavored it with berries, seeds, or dried meat.

Native Americans had their own religion. They worshipped the Creators. The Creators gave them all the things in nature that they needed to live. The people trusted religious leaders called **shamans**. The shamans explained the world to the people. They led religious services, located food, and healed the sick. During religious services, the people gave thanks to the Creators with songs, music, and dance. They also thanked the Creators daily by respecting nature.

Yuman-speakers used rattles made of deer hooves in religious ceremonies.

San Diego has a fine harbor.

STRANGERS ARRIVE

During the 1500s, Spanish explorers came to southwestern California. One explorer was Juan Rodríguez Cabrillo. In 1542, Cabrillo claimed the area for Spain. He did not care that the land belonged to the American Indians living there. In 1602, another Spanish explorer named the area San Diego. Then Spain seemed to forget about the area.

In the mid-1700s, Spanish king Carlos III decided the land should be protected for Spain. He ordered explorers, soldiers, and missionaries to the new land. Once there, they were to start farming. The Spaniards planned ways to make the American Indians living there follow the Spanish and become workers. They also planned to teach the American Indians about the Catholic faith.

Missions seemed the best way to do this. Father Junípero Serra led the mission plan. Beginning in San Diego, Father Serra was to build missions as far north as what would become Monterey. If the plan worked, these missions would one day become Spanish pueblos.

Father Serra founded the first mission in San Diego, in 1769.

THE FIRST MISSION

In 1769, a group of 219 settlers left Spanish settlements in what later became Mexico. They traveled north to San

Diego by land and sea. The journey was hard. Many settlers got sick. Only half of the group survived the trip.

Father Serra and the other Spaniards scouted the San Diego area. They chose a spot for a settlement. It was not far from the Yuman-speaking village of Cosoy. The missionaries and soldiers built brush and soil shelters and a church. On July 16, 1769, Father Serra held Catholic mass. This religious service officially founded Mission San Diego de Alcalá. It was California's first mission.

Mission San
Diego de Alcalá

·2·

MISSIONS OF THE SOUTHERN COAST

Three missions make up California's southern coast missions. They are missions San Diego de Alcalá, San Luis Rey de Francia, and San Juan Capistrano. The presidio at the port of San Diego protected the southern coast missions.

Each mission has its own history. Each is a reminder of California's past. San Diego de Alcalá had more difficulty getting started than other missions. Founders had to deal with poor soil, and local people attacked the mission. San Juan Capistrano did well from its founding. San Luis Rey de Francia also flourished.

MISSION SAN DIEGO DE ALCALÁ

Father Serra thought the San Diego site was a good one when he chose it in 1769. There was water to drink. There were plants and animals to eat. But the nearby San Diego River soon dried up. The plants died. The animals left. The Spaniards had to send a ship back to Mexico for supplies.

Father Serra's troubles continued. He tried to teach the Catholic faith to the Yuman-speaking people. But it was hard for the two groups to trust each other. Their different languages made it hard to understand each other. The Spaniards did not respect Native American ways of life. The American Indians were angry that the Spanish had taken their lands. They also felt upset that the Spaniards hunted the animals they needed for food.

Father Serra tried to make friends with the American

A priest baptizes a Native American baby. This ceremony welcomed the baby into the Catholic Church.

Indians. He offered them goods, such as cloth and beads. Some American Indians decided to join the mission. But most of them remained angry at the Spaniards. They did not want to follow the Spanish way of life. They wanted the Spaniards to leave.

The Native Americans attacked the mission to get their land back. Their revolt failed. Three Native Americans lost their lives. Many others were hurt. One Spaniard died.

After the battle, there was a shaky peace between the Native Americans and the Spaniards. But food and water were still scarce. The Spaniards were running out of supplies. The supply ship had not arrived. In January 1770, Captain Gaspar de Portolá entered the mission. He was a Spanish military leader. He ordered the mission closed. But Father Serra convinced him the supply ship would come. In March, the ship arrived. Mission San Diego de Alcalá could continue.

Captain Gaspar de Portolá leads Spanish soldiers.

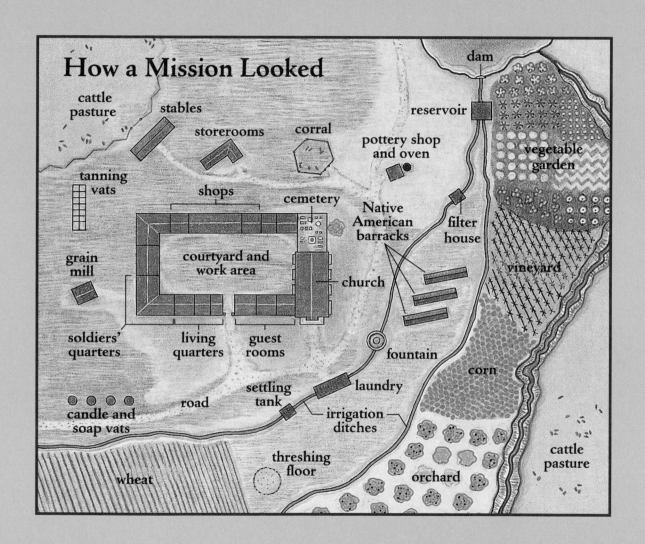

How a Mission Looked

cattle pasture

stables

storerooms

corral

dam

reservoir

pottery shop and oven

vegetable garden

tanning vats

shops

cemetery

Native American barracks

filter house

grain mill

courtyard and work area

church

vineyard

soldiers' quarters

living quarters

guest rooms

fountain

corn

candle and soap vats

road

settling tank

laundry

irrigation ditches

cattle pasture

wheat

threshing floor

orchard

MISSION LIFE

Mission San Diego de Alcalá began to take shape in early 1770. Soldiers and missionaries replaced the original mission buildings with sturdier ones. Father Serra decided the mission was established enough for him to leave. Father Luís Jayme took Father Serra's place.

More Native Americans came to the mission in the next few years. They came seeking food and treatment for sickness. The missionaries made the Native Americans stay in exchange for help. The missionaries taught the neophytes the Spanish language and the Catholic religion. They also taught the neophytes how to farm. The neophytes worked in mission fields.

Spanish soldiers at the nearby presidio did not treat the neophytes well. Father Jayme decided to move the mission away from the presidio. In 1774, the priest established the mission a few miles away on the San Diego River. The soil was good in the new location. Crops began to thrive. More Native Americans came to the new mission for food.

By 1774, the missionaries and neophytes had built many

At the missions, neophytes farmed the land.

buildings on the new site. They built a church. They built homes. They put up a granary for storing grain. They placed the buildings around the four sides of an open, square patio. This building plan is called a **quadrangle.**

MORE CONFLICT

Native American leaders were worried that so many members were leaving the villages. They saw that their way of life was disappearing. The leaders also saw that the Spaniards were taking their lands to grow crops.

At midnight on November 4, 1775, 800 Yuman-speaking people attacked San Diego de Alcalá. They set fire to the mission buildings. They killed Father Jayme. They destroyed the mission.

REBUILDING

The Spanish did not give up. Missionaries and neophytes rebuilt the mission. Spanish leaders sent more soldiers to the mission to protect it and to control the Native Americans. The Native Americans' way of life was disappearing.

The mission grew. In 1797, the mission population was higher than any other California mission. The neophytes worked as farmers and ranchers. Their work helped make San Diego de Alcalá one of California's most productive missions.

Neophytes rebuilt parts of Mission San Diego de Alcalá. They made a bell tower.

❖❖❖

MISSION SAN JUAN CAPISTRANO

Mission San Juan Capistrano is north of San Diego de Alcalá. The mission was founded twice. Father Serra asked Father Fermín Francisco de Lasuén to choose a site for the mission. In 1775, Father Lasuén began building San Juan Capistrano in what became Orange County.

Shoshonean-speaking people in the area helped the missionaries with the building. But after eight days of work, problems at San Diego de Alcalá stopped the project. Father Lasuén buried the church bells. He went to help at the mission to the south.

In 1776, Father Serra returned to the mission. Father Serra, two other priests, and 22 soldiers dug up the bells. They started building the mission again. Native Americans helped with the building. The church was the first structure the builders completed. They named it Serra's Chapel.

The mission grew quickly. By 1778, 150 neophytes were living and working there. In 1784, the neophyte

Many people consider San Juan Capistrano one of the most beautiful missions.

population reached 550. They received food, shelter, and training. But they weren't paid. Their hard work made San Juan Capistrano a beautiful mission.

MAKING ADOBE AND BUILDING MISSIONS

There were few trees in southern California. The missionaries had to build with something other than wood. They taught the neophytes to make clay bricks called **adobe**.

The neophytes made adobe by mixing clay soil with sand, water, and straw. They cut the mixture into rectangular bricks.

To make walls, neophytes stacked bricks of adobe.

Then they dried the bricks in the sun. The bricks were excellent building blocks. The missionaries told the neophytes what to build with the blocks.

Missionaries created building plans for the neophytes to follow. They told neophytes where to stack adobe to make walls. Roofs were made of wood and clay tiles. The neophytes made the tiles by drying sheets of clay in ovens called **kilns**. Neophytes also painted buildings with a mixture made of lime (a white powder), salt, and goat's milk.

The workers at San Juan Capistrano followed a quadrangle building plan. Serra's Chapel formed one wall of the structure. Living quarters and other buildings formed the remaining walls. People had to build buildings outside the quadrangle as the mission grew.

A NEW CHURCH

In the 1770s, Serra's Chapel became too small for the mission population. The missionaries drew up a plan for a stone church. The church would be cross shaped. It would have a domed ceiling and a high tower.

In 1797, neophytes began cutting and setting stone. In 1799, a stone worker named Isídro Aguilár arrived at the mission. He showed the neophytes how to build with stone.

Aguilár died in 1803. But the neophytes had learned well. They kept building. They finished the structure three years later. It could seat more than 1,000 people. Its bells could be heard from miles away. The missionaries called the new building the Great Stone Church.

The Great Stone Church *(right)* was a large building with plenty of room for worshippers.

THE MISSION CRUMBLES

On December 8, 1812, an earthquake shook San Juan Capistrano. The great tower fell. It crashed into the church roof. Nearly 40 neophytes were crushed inside the church. The church was too damaged to use again. Services were held in Serra's Chapel once again.

The earthquake also damaged the rest of the mission. Neophytes worked to fix the buildings.

But illness swept through the mission. Many neophytes died. With fewer workers, Mission San Juan Capistrano began to fail.

An 1812 earthquake at the Great Stone Church made the church's roof fall in.

◆◆◆

Mission San Luis Rey de Francia

Father Serra founded nine missions before he died in 1784. Father Lasuén took over Father Serra's job as head of the mission system. In 1798, he chose an area between San Diego de Alcalá and San Juan Capistrano. The area would be the site of San Luis Rey de Francia.

The area was in a valley. Water flowed from the nearby San Luis Rey River. The area also had underground streams called springs. The water supply made the valley green with plant life.

Native American leaders did not fully welcome the Spaniards. But the missionaries offered them gifts. The leaders came to accept the Spanish. Within months, 214 neophytes lived and worked at the mission.

FATHER PEYRI

Father Antonio Peyri was a priest at San Luis Rey de Francia. He led the mission for 33 years.

Father Peyri ran Mission San Luis Rey for more than 30 years.

The mission flourished under Father Peyri. He created several building projects and a trade system.

The mission quadrangle was bigger than a modern football field. The design of the mission chapel was based on the Great Stone Church. The church held more than 1,000 people. The chapel and quadrangle sat above many fruit trees and fields of grain. Some people thought the mission looked like a palace.

Father Peyri was clever. One of his building projects was a *lavandería* (laundry area) that used valuable water twice. The lavandería sat in a valley in front of the mission. Water from an underground stream

Father Peyri created a laundry area in which water traveled downward beside stone steps *(top)* into a pool *(middle)*. Women used the water to wash clothes. The water then went through a filter *(bottom)* before flowing to the mission's gardens.

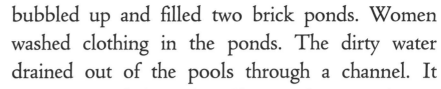

Neophytes decorated this holy-water basin. They dipped their right hands in the basin before church services.

bubbled up and filled two brick ponds. Women washed clothing in the ponds. The dirty water drained out of the pools through a channel. It passed through a filter to clean it. Then it flowed out to water the mission's gardens.

DAILY LIFE

Life at San Luis Rey was like that at other missions. The missionaries and neophytes kept a daily schedule. The ringing of bells signaled different parts of the day's schedule.

Bells at sunrise called the neophytes to morning church services. The bells rang again to signal breakfast. One hour later, bells called the neophytes to work. Noon bells signaled when it was time for lunch. After lunch came siesta, when everyone rested for two hours. Next, bells called the neophytes back to work. Bells also signaled the day's end.

Work at the missions was hard. Neophytes worked all day. Some made shoes, wove cloth, and shaped adobe bricks. Many neophytes worked in the fields. They plowed the fields and planted crops. Other neophytes worked with livestock. They milked cows, branded cattle, or sheared sheep.

MISSION TRADE

Father Peyri and the neophytes created a system of trade. They traded the goods produced at the mission for goods

San Luis Rey de Francia produced many goods. The mission traded these goods for goods brought by supply ships.

they needed. Spain had forbidden the missionaries from trading with other countries. Spain did not want non-Spanish people to come to the area. But Father Peyri saw he had to trade to get goods for the mission. So he traded items with sailors whose ships sailed the Pacific coast. He traded for iron tools, needles, buttons, and books.

San Luis Rey de Francia was very successful. By the 1820s, the mission owned 28,000 sheep, 22,000 cattle, and 1,500 horses. It produced more fruits and grains than it could use and trade. Father Peyri gave some of his mission's goods to other missions.

Father Peyri had many plans for the mission. But by the late 1820s, Spain was losing control of its land in California. Father Peyri knew his dreams for the mission would probably not come true.

By the early 1820s, San Luis Rey de Francia was one of the largest missions.

❖ 3 ❖

STATE CONTROL OF THE MISSIONS

The early 1800s were a time of trouble for Spain. The country was fighting a war in Europe. It could not support its soldiers or settlers in California.

But the missions were doing well. The soldiers and settlers soon became angry that priests controlled the missions. The soldiers and settlers wanted mission lands for themselves.

NEW THREATS

In 1821, Mexico gained its freedom from Spain. Mexico claimed the territory of California. It created laws that gave greater freedom to many. This included Native Americans.

Spanish settlers and non-Spanish settlers joined together. They called themselves Californios. They pleaded with the Mexican government to **secularize** the missions. This policy would put the missions under state, or government, control. It would force the missionaries to give up the missions. Then the missions' land could be divided up and given to Californios.

The missionaries fought the secularization plan but lost. The Mexican government put the missions in control of local leaders. The leaders replaced the missionaries with Mexican priests. Father Peyri stayed to fight the plan as long as he could. He finally left in 1832.

LIFE AT THE MISSIONS

In 1833, the Mexican government started its plan of secularization. It first secularized San Luis Rey. It secularized San Juan Capistrano in the same year. The

Father Peyri stands on deck as his ship pulls away from the coast in 1832.

neophytes received only some of the land. The rest of the land was given to Californios. Without workers, San Juan Capistrano quickly fell apart.

Mexico secularized San Diego de Alcalá in 1834. Mexican leader José Figueroa met with the neophytes to free them personally. Some Native Americans decided to

Some ex-neophytes had a hard time making a living

stay with the missionaries at the missions. Others chose to live in Native American communities. Californios took much of San Diego de Alcalá's land.

The Californios used the lands from the missions to create **ranchos**. The Californios wanted even more land for these ranches. They pressured ex-neophytes with land to sell it. The Californios often did not pay the Native Americans fairly for the land.

CIVIL ADMINISTRATORS

The Mexican government named civil administrators. These citizen leaders were to oversee the change in ownership of mission lands. They were to make sure old mission lands were divided fairly. But most of the administrators were unfair to ex-neophytes.

The administrators forced ex-neophytes to work on ranchos. The ex-neophytes received little or no pay. The administrators gave away mission lands to family and friends.

A civil administrator talks to ex-neophytes at San Luis Rey.

They misused mission property. Some stole from the missions.

In 1845, an administrator named Pío Pico became governor of the territory. He decided that all the missions should be sold or rented. He sold San Juan Capistrano to his brother-in-law. He granted San Luis Rey to other family members. A friend of Pico bought San Diego de Alcalá.

Pío Pico gained a large amount of land that had once belonged to missions.

The missions no longer produced the goods they once had. The ranchos mainly produced beef and leather. These goods were sold to the United States. Rancho owners became rich. But Native Americans became poor.

U.S. TAKEOVER

In the early 1840s, the United States offered to buy the California territory. But Mexico refused the offer. The two countries argued over the area for several years. In 1846, the United States went to war with Mexico. Mexico lost

Ex-neophytes sometimes worked for people who had taken over mission land.

the Mexican War in 1848. The U.S. government took control of the California territory. The territory became a state two years later.

Many people from the eastern United States moved to California. The people wanted land to live on and farm. In the 1850s, the U.S. government passed new laws. The laws said that Californios had to prove that lands were theirs. They had to go to court and convince officials that the land really belonged to them.

The Californios knew that they could not prove ownership. The U.S. government honored the easterners' claims to the lands. In time, the U.S. government moved some Native Americans to lands set aside for them. But these **reservations** were often on land that was not good for hunting, gathering, or farming.

MISSION BUILDINGS

The new U.S. settlers cared little for the missions. Most went unused. They fell apart.

The U.S. Army housed soldiers at San Luis Rey and San Diego de Alcalá. The soldiers tore down parts of the church at San Luis Rey. At San Diego de Alcalá, the soldiers added a second floor to the church. They lived on this new floor. They kept their horses on the first floor. Ranchers stored hay in Serra's Chapel at San Juan Capistrano.

The weather damaged the adobe walls of San Diego de Alcalá.

These broken-down arches at San Juan Capistrano show how neglected the missions were.

The U.S. government returned the missions to the Roman Catholic Church. During the 1850s and the 1860s, priests tried to fix the missions. But they did not have enough money. It seemed that no one could save the missions.

San Diego de Alcalá,
about 1905

THE MISSIONS IN MODERN TIMES

By the late 1800s, it seemed most people had lost interest in the missions. But a few artists still cared about them. They painted pictures and took photos of the missions. They wrote stories about them. People in the United States saw the beauty of the missions. They enjoyed reading about their history.

In 1895, writer Charles F. Lummis took action. He organized the Landmarks Club. This group raised money to fix the missions and other historical buildings.

SAN JUAN CAPISTRANO

The Landmarks Club decided to rebuild San Juan Capistrano. Putting a new roof on Serra's Chapel was the group's first project. Workers also strengthened the walls of the Great Stone Church.

The Landmarks Club quit rebuilding the missions in 1917. Catholic priests took over repairing the missions. Father John O'Sullivan wanted to work on San Juan Capistrano.

Serra's Chapel was almost rubble when the Landmarks Club stepped in to rebuild it.

Father O'Sullivan stands in San Juan Capistrano's courtyard

Father O'Sullivan lived and worked at the mission. Life was hard there at first. The buildings were full of fleas. Father O'Sullivan had to stay in a tent. He worked alone.

The priest had an idea. He charged visitors to see the mission. He used the money to buy supplies. Father O'Sullivan also hired workers. In 1917, Father O'Sullivan and the workers finished their project. People came to worship at Serra's Chapel.

SAN LUIS REY DE FRANCIA

San Luis Rey was empty until 1892. Then a group of Mexican priests wanted to start a school to train new priests. They thought San Luis Rey was a good place for their **seminary**.

Catholic leaders said the priests could use the mission. They put Father Joseph O'Keefe in charge of the school. He and the Mexican priests rebuilt the church roof. They

patched the cracked dome. Men came to the school.

In 1903, the Mexican priests left the school. Father O'Keefe stayed to run the seminary and restore the mission. The priest rebuilt the quadrangle. He made it smaller but stronger than the original.

The buildings and seminary lasted. Students and priests continued to repair the mission over the years. They searched for old building remains and fixed them. Today the mission is a center for religious groups.

SAN DIEGO DE ALCALÁ

By the early 1900s, most buildings at San Diego de Alcalá were unsafe. The U.S. Army tore down many of these structures. The rest of the mission buildings were a school for American Indians.

In 1931, the citizens of San Diego wanted to restore the mission. They raised money to fix it. Workers found the original mission bell. They repaired buildings. They planted trees and a garden.

By the late 1980s, San Diego de Alcalá was a flourishing church. More than 1,700 families worshipped there. Church leaders decided they needed more room. They decided to build a new meeting hall.

Tourists visit San Diego de Alcalá in the early 1900s.

There was a problem with the area leaders chose for the hall. It was a cemetery. American Indians were buried there. People were angry that leaders wanted to build there. In 1989, church leaders decided to build the hall in a different place at the mission.

THE SOUTHERN COAST MISSIONS TODAY

The three southern coast missions are busy churches. They are also museums. The past and the present come together at the missions.

The citizens of San Juan Capistrano make their mission an important part of their town. They continue to raise money to repair the mission. Recently they added a new church. Workers built this church from original plans of the Great Stone Church. Visitors can see swallows at San Juan Capistrano. These birds migrate to the area in the spring.

Student groups often visit the missions of the southern coast.

San Luis Rey de Francia now stands in the city of Oceanside. Visitors can walk the steps of the lavandería. They can learn about the American Indians who lived and worked at the mission. A museum displays Father Peyri's robes.

San Diego de Alcalá is a peaceful place in the busy port city of San Diego. It has rich, colorful plant and flower gardens. Travelers can visit the American Indian cemetery there.

LAYOUTS

These diagrams of California's southern coast missions show what the missions look like in modern times. Modern-day missions may not look exactly like the original missions Spanish priests founded. But by studying them, we can get a sense of how neophytes and missionaries lived.

San Diego de Alcalá:

Father Junípero Serra founded this mission on July 16, 1769. It was the first church in California. People still attend church at the mission in modern times.

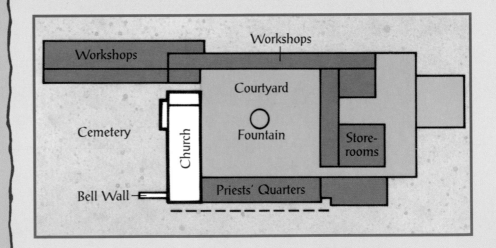

San Juan Capistrano:

This mission was established on November 1, 1776. It is most famous for its cliff swallows. These birds migrate to the area every spring.

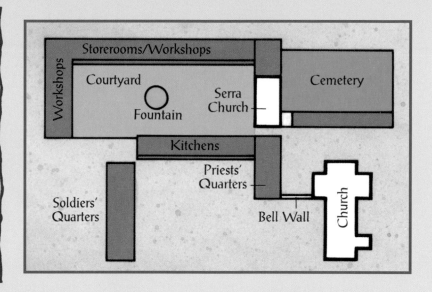

San Luis Rey de Francia:

This mission was founded on June 13, 1798. Today, visitors to the mission can tour the grounds, visit a museum, or attend a church service.

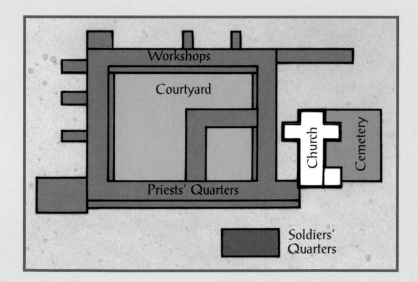

TIMELINE

1542   Juan Rodríguez Cabrillo claims San Diego Bay for Spain

1769   Father Junípero Serra founds San Diego de Alcalá

1775   Native Americans rebel at Mission San Diego; San Juan Capistrano is founded and abandoned

1776   San Juan Capistrano is reestablished

1784   Father Serra dies; Father Fermín Francisco de Lasuén becomes the new father-president

1798   San Luis Rey de Francia is founded

1812   An earthquake strikes San Juan Capistrano

1821   Mexico gains freedom from Spain

1833   The Mexican government begins to secularize the missions

1846   Mexican War begins between Mexico and the United States

1848   Mexican War ends; the United States gains control of California

1850   California becomes the thirty-first state

       The U.S. government begins to return the California missions to the Roman Catholic Church; mission buildings are falling apart

1890   Mission restorations begin; they continue through present times

GLOSSARY

adobe: bricks made by mixing clay soil with sand, water, and straw

bands: groups of Native Americans who live together. Shoshonean- and Yuman-speaking Native Americans lived in bands.

kilns: ovens for drying clay. Neophytes made roofing tiles by drying sheets of clay in kilns.

mesas: flat-topped hills

missionaries: teachers sent out by religious groups to spread their religion to others

missions: centers where religious teachers work to spread their beliefs to other people

neophytes: Native Americans who have joined the Roman Catholic faith and community

presidios: Spanish forts for housing soldiers

pueblos: towns

quadrangle: an area or patio surrounded by buildings on four sides

ranchos: ranches. Californios used land from the missions to create ranchos.

reservations: areas of land the U.S. government set aside for use by Native Americans

secularize: to transfer from missionary to state control. When the missions were secularized, they were no longer controlled by the church.

seminary: a school where men train to become priests

shamans: Native American religious leaders

PRONUNCIATION GUIDE*

Cabrillo, Juan Rodríguez	kah-BREE-yoh, WAHN roh-DREE-gehz
El Camino Reál	el kah-MEE-no ray-AHL
Jayme, Luís	HY-may, loo-EES
Lasuén, Fermín Francisco de	lah-soo-AYN, fair-MEEN frahn-SEES-koh day
Peyri, Antonio	PAY-ree, ahn-TOH-nee-oh
Portolá, Gaspar de	por-toh-LAH, gahs-PAHR day
San Diego de Alcalá	SAHN dee-AY-go day ahl-kah-LAH
San Juan Capistrano	SAHN WAHN kay-pees-TRAH-noh
San Luis Rey de Francia	SAHN loo-EES RAY day FRAHN-see-ah
Serra, Junípero	SEH-rrah, hoo-NEE-pay-roh

* Local pronunciations may differ

TO LEARN MORE

Behrens, June. *Central Coast Missions in California.* Minneapolis: Lerner Publications, 2008. Learn all about the missions of California's central coast.

Mission Basilica San Diego de Alcalá http://www.missionsandiego.com/ San Diego de Alcalá's website features detailed information on the mission. It also includes a special section for fourth-graders who are studying missions.

Mission San Juan Capistrano http://www.missionsjc.com/ Visit San Juan Capistrano's official website to read more about the history of this southern coast mission.

Mission San Luis Rey http://www.sanluisrey.org/ San Luis Rey de Francia's site includes historical information and a section especially for students.

Nelson, Libby, and Kari A. Cornell. *California Mission Projects and Layouts.* Minneapolis: Lerner Publications, 2008. This book provides guides for building mission models. It also offers layouts of California's 21 missions.

Sonneborn, Liz. *The Chumash.* Minneapolis: Lerner Publications, 2007. This book introduces the Chumash, Native Americans whose homeland is in California.

Van Steenwyk, Elizabeth. *The California Missions.* New York: Franklin Watts, 1995. Van Steenwyk introduces California missions through clear text and full-color photographs.

INDEX